Seeds of Tears

Harvest of Joy

A Journey Through Grief

Fabian E. Sanchez

Dedicated to the memory of my dear aunt,

Andrea Maria Davis

August 16, 1965 – February 20, 2023

Tears, groans, and sighs …

We could never have seen this coming, yet here we are. April fools' day, the day of your funeral. Yet, none is fooled as we face the reality of your *passing. A beautiful light has left our lives, leaving us in the darkness of grief.*

In our last conversation via WhatsApp, you relayed how your first clinic appointment was, post three weeks from hospital discharge. You shared that the Doctor didn't recognize you. In your words, "him say me look very, very nice. Him say me look new." We could never have imagined that shortly thereafter, things would have taken the turn they did. Never in my wildest dreams would I have thought upon picking you up that fateful afternoon of Monday February 20th, to head to the hospital that you would be taken from us three hours later.

Alas, thank you for the message in the dream on the morning of Ash Wednesday. When asked by those in the afterlife "What are you doing here?" you responded, "I knew nothing was going to change." Nothing might have changed, but indeed it did, to the Glory of God! You have a new home in the heavenly realm. Watch over us and intercede

for us!

Table of Contents

Introduction

In **Seeds of Tears Harvest of Joy**, the author calls upon contemplative, poetic and philosophical underpinnings as he availed himself to the process of grieving, from which this anthology emerged. Drawing on the created world around him, he journeyed with grief, as he sought to make sense of life, while facing loss. He considers his own mortality, the unnegotiable needs of life in the face of all its vanity, while not abandoning hope, faith, and love; the things that will last.

You are invited to take this journey of contemplation alongside the author, as you journey through grief, as you seek to come to terms with the desolation it brings, and your struggle to emerge from its grip. Each entry presents a perspective which you are invited to internalize as you read, pausing after each reflection to harvest your joy as a supplement to boost your continued journey through what is a difficult life experience.

Look's Deception

"Him say me look very, very nice, him say me look new." There is a deception that attends our appearance at times. One that fails to betray the turmoil that is happening within, showing no signs of an informer via symptoms. Its proverbial mouth locked shut, only to speak when it is too late, and the damage is already done. A damage beyond the powers of medicine to correct. A damage that even a miracle avoids.

And so, it is true, a book judged by its cover leads to your self-deception. Within its pages, lie the true story. A story not discernable from its cover, however very, very nice it looks.

Be aware of looks deception.

Pause and Harvest….

Are you deceived by a look? Consider your own life or that of a loved one. Is there something that should be explored concerning your health, or theirs? Is there some action you must take but have been avoiding same?

Remember, time lost can never be regained. It is time for you to act. Now!

Dreams to Remember, Dreams to Prepare Us

If you are like me, then your dreams don't often make much sense as you try to recall and interpret what they might mean. Yet, there may be one, two or several that after certain events occur, the mind somehow recalls the dream and you are forced to stop and ponder, could this be what that dream meant?

In the wake of my aunt's passing, I was forced to come to terms with a dream remembered, one that seemed to have been intended to grant me a window into what was to come. You see, my aunt was a lover of mangoes, and in the dream, or the vision which came to me while I slept, I saw her in what could have been a scene from a tragic movie. In this scene, she was calling out to someone, reminding them to bring the mangoes to her, something she would usually do during mango season, her loves being Blackie, Julie and East Indian, although where mangoes were concerned for her, there was no discrimination. The scene quickly transitioned to her being on a tree, a guinep tree, one that sits on a section of the property at home, which overlooked the neighbour's yard below. As if fortuitous, foretelling what was to come, the limb of the tree on which she was perched began to break. She fell from the tree. The scene transitioned to me running towards where she fell. Like a premonition, hours later that Sunday morning I was to receive a call from the hospital, summoning me there immediately as my aunt was in distress. The events which followed, after treatment, gave us hope of a brighter tomorrow. However, unbeknownst to us, it was to have been only a reprieve, the dream to remember, to prepare us was not to be undone, the scene scrapped.

Alas! Our dreams, visions even, have meaning. If we are present enough, the events of our lives will make them plain for us to see. Beforehand or in retrospect, they will either prepare us, or make plain in retrospect what our veiled eyes could not see.

Pause and Harvest…

Is there a dream, a vision that you have had, or been having? Though at times our dreams and visions are never discernable, and we even forget them as soon as we awake, our subconscious will always recall. Think back to a time when something happened, and your subconscious presented you with the foretelling of that manifestation in the dream/vision you would have had.

Now pay heed to those dreams/visions! To borrow a phrase from the cartoon Thundercats, and the Sword of Omens, your dreams/visions are "sight beyond sight."

Our Grand Act

And the essence of life is to take care of each other for the time we have here, in this space and time with each other.

The stage that is life will see our loved ones making their exits, leaving us to carry on until our act has ended and we too leave the stage.

As it is said in show business, the show must go on, even amidst tragedy. The momentum that is life will not be suspended for you and I to catch our breath or even compose ourselves. It simply carries on amidst our turmoil, until we are able to mellow, while we continue to trod along the path it has in store for us, in our grand act of showmanship.

All the world's a stage. Life is a stage. We must keep acting until our final curtain call.

Pause and Harvest...

Amidst all the cares of life, are you taking care of you in order to take care of those who depend on you? Where does your focus rest; on things, people, or places? Which carries the utmost importance for you, when the rubber hits the road?

Thief

And just like that death steals your loved ones like a thief. No army of guards can prevent its breaching of our perimeter fences, burglar bars or high-tech alarm systems. Its invisible tentacles reach in and takes whom it wishes, when it wishes, how it wishes. No consent sought, no permission needed, no notice given. It simply reaps, as if sowed at birth. It simply collects like a bailiff charged to recover on a bad debt. It takes what belongs to it. It is a reaper of life, of souls.

Pause and Harvest...

The imagery of the thief who comes unannounced serves as a poignant point of reference, calling us to consider what provision we have made should the unknown hour of our demise appear.

Make that will! Take out that life insurance policy for those who might need the support when you are no longer around. Make those provisions that only you can. We are truly not invincible nor were we made to last.

Earth Pains

Does the earth hurt when we trample upon it? Does it bleed when we dig into it with our hoes, pickaxes, tractors, and excavators? Does it feel? Does it cry, does it holla at the pains it bears from our hands? Is it alive yet lifeless? Alive to spring forth. Feed us, clothe us, enrich us, enslave us, and free us. Inflict its own pains on us. Its own emotional turmoil like payback just because it can as part of its course.

Like wine mingled with vinegar, we are left to drink from its cup, mingle in earth pains of joy and sadness, triumph, and defeat. Misery and happiness. Inescapable we are from the grasp of Earth Pains. Pains we must endure, while courageously carrying on.

Pause and Harvest…

Pain seems to be an inescapable part of our existence. Our mothers birth us through the pain of childbirth, and throughout our lives we must endure painful experiences. Alas, like a child emerging from its mother's womb, painful an experience as it is for a mother, it also brings great joy.

Consider your painful experiencies and how you have emerged joyfully through them. Now, envision emerging joyfully from your present journey through grief.

5.7 on the Richter Scale

You're like a massive earthquake that destroys one's entire life's possessions, where there is no insurance to help pick up the pieces and rebuild. You leave us with a great void, an emptiness, the carpet pulled from under our feet, a profound sense of loss, left to face the ruins of the life we once knew, cherished, and loved. You're a demolisher! You give us no plan, no coping mechanism, no instructional guide. Forcing us to go through the process of rising, overcoming, letting go, healing, coming to terms with our loss, relinquishing any sense of control we deceive ourselves into believing we have, forcing us to go on, our lives having suffered a major disruption in the wake of your shake.

Pause and Harvest...

If you have experienced an earthquake from wherever you are in the world, you know how frightening it can be, as well as the massive destruction it can cause. Having survived an earthquake, we must look to the future. Consider the ways you can move forward even amidst loss and other challenges. It may not feel like it now, but truly, there is light at the end of every tunnel.

Triggering Events....

At times we are guilty of making or finding ourselves on the receiving end of statements/comments said innocently. The speaker of such comments is sometimes oblivious that their words are like pressure applied to an unhealed wound which disturbs the recipient's mental state, momentarily or otherwise. As the recipient, we must be able to recognize these triggering events so as not to allow them to derail our mental state or drive us into a state of being discombobulated or depressed. Very few may be aware of the mental battles we fight. As such, it is up to you and me to recognize those triggers and rise above them.

Pause and Harvest…

What are some ways I can improve my self-awareness?

Transitioning

There is something surreal about seeing the people you grew up around ageing; afflicted with the challenges of the accumulation of years. Becoming frail and even childlike in appearance, speech, and demeanor. The adage once a man twice a child becoming real and appreciable. Leads to the contemplation of readying oneself to journey with your loved ones through the process, the transitioning of generations. In the end, our journeys are not dissimilar. We all, if graced with long life, must ready ourselves for our own journey of transitioning. When that time comes may we have the warmth of our loved ones around us.

Pause and Harvest…

How have I benefitted from the wisdom of my fore parents and how am I creating and translating my family traditions and customs to inform the generation I will leave behind?

The Answer

Life at times presents us with haunting memories of things seen, unexplained by the explanations sought, leaving us in the dark to deal with and overcome unanswered questions. There is a darkness we must contend with, which cannot be illuminated. Certainly not in the physical. Even with science and the great strides that man's pursuit of knowledge has equipped him to unearth, the answers given at times will not support the evidence of that which his eyes have seen. There are those occasions in which the explanations may concur with the manifestation, the fruit of sickness. Where it doesn't, the mysteries of life remain impenetrable, and we must overcome the desire to know that which seems encapsulated in a darkness like the deepest parts of the ocean where sunlight will never descend.

You and I as we journey the road of grief, are challenged to train our minds to make peace with that darkness which hides the answers to the questions we seek. Closure will not always be possible in the physical. The answers we seek might reside in the land we are yet to possess, inhabit.

Pause and Harvest...

What questions do I have, the answers for which are nowhere in sight?

Is it time to release those questions and the desire to have them answered?

How do I find peace in not knowing?

The Way of Grief, the Way of the Cross

For people of faith, particularly within Christendom, they would be all too familiar with the crucifixion story of Jesus. A story that was sorrowful throughout, to its ultimate end. They would also be familiar with scriptural reference which reminds them that having been baptized in Christ Jesus, they were baptized into his death and his resurrection. Symbolic in the immersing of the body in water and the rising to new life from its depts.

Amidst a sorrowful evening along the unfolding journey of grief, it was registered in my consciousness that the Way of Grief can be likened to the Way of the Cross. If truly the baptized is buried in death with Christ, to rise with him in glory, then the experience of grief as experienced by Jesus, his disciples, his mother and the women closest to him, along the way of the cross to his crucifixion, encapsulated in the depts of its sorrowful experience, can be likened to our own experience of grief occasioned by the death of a loved one. Like Jesus' disciples, we were followers of our beloved unto death. Like parties to a crime, we are parties to grief. Parties to the way of the cross.

Pause and Harvest…

Is there a place for faith in your life? If so, how has it been serving you? If not, would it make a difference in your experience of living?

Mortality

The man who breathes and considers not his mortality must be immortal.

Death, our inescapable companion follows us around, like our shadow reflecting in the presence of sunlight it stands. Stands waiting to serve its purpose, aided, and abetted by pestilence, diseases, underlying conditions and disasters of earthly or human creation. We walk and live in its shadow. Ignoring it often we do, whilst it is ever mindful of our goings and comings. Fear it we do not! Fear us it does not! Yet, we live at its mercy as it numbers our days while we pray our days are unnumbered.

Our shadow, death, smirks at us having ate from the tree of knowledge, holding the keys to our breath of life. Numbers he the hour when he shall strike. Our end in sight by the snipers might.

Pause and Harvest...

When last did you consider your mortality? How does it, or has it shaped your living?

Introspection

As we grow and grow older, we can at times get trapped in the deception that comes with assessing our life and our journey with what we perceive, real and imagined, to be in the lives of others that is lacking in ours. Often, we lose sight of the fact that the grass isn't always greener on the other side and further, all that glitters isn't gold. Without the wisdom to reside in the blessings, the uniqueness of our own circumstances and our own journey, we would forever be inadequate in the face of comparison. Our joy sapped, our spirit broken, living in the land of the lack we experience looking into the window of another, rather than basting in all that we have within the house that is ours.

May we all be happy and content with the image we see in the mirror each day.

May we work to change the things we can, born from our own dreams, desires and aspirations. May we pray for the wisdom to accept those things we cannot change and the grace to know the difference.

May our joy and spirit never be sapped by the thief of comparison.

May we embrace all that we are and live while relishing the beauty of the grass on our side of the fence. May we entrust all that we are in our brokenness to the mercy of a judge who knows our heart. And in the end, may we like the thief on the cross rejoice in paradise, whatever our belief of paradise is.

Pause and Harvest…

Are you among those who see the glass as being half empty as opposed to half full?

Are you playing the game of unhealthy comparison?

Are you seeing the lawn of your neighbor as being greener, yet not watering your own lawn to achieve a greener outcome?

How will you make a change for the better?

No Reprieve

Amid life, there is indeed death. Yet, life stops not for you nor I, when death walks in to disturb what was our equilibrium. Nothing stops the wheels of life from turning or its clock from ticking. The living must simply continue to live. Afterall, life is just for living they say.

Life is left to the living, death to the dead. Worlds apart they are. Yet in our humanness connected. The reality of the latter often leaves the living in despondency. Yet, forced to carry-on. What else can the living do but live, even while faced with the despondency occasioned by the death of a loved one. The insensitivity of life. It bids you to simply, carry-on.

Pause and Harvest...

What is my why? Consider the many 'whys' you have to carry-on.

In case you need a why, you are alive and your only choice is to live.

Tears and Sunshine

The process of grieving manifests itself like a storm. Only, there is no forecasting to allow you to prepare for the deluge of tears that you are likely to shed sometimes when you least expected to. The clouds of this storm build, and its saturation is released by the slightest of thought, memory of your beloved, acting as a prick which occasions the flow from the dam of one's eyes.

Somewhere on the other side of this storm of tears, you'll find sunshine. The clouds saturated with tears won't always persist. Storms are but for a moment in time; but while they do exist, endure in the sure hope that it will become a little less when the sun appears to dry up your hurricane-soaked sheets of tears.

Rain of tears today. Maybe rays of sunshine tomorrow. Embrace each as it comes.

Pause and Harvest...

What precious memories of your loved one do you hold dare?

Let these memories strengthen and empower you to move ahead. They are no longer with you physically, but in spirit, they are.

Eternal Life, Eternal Spirit

There must be something more to this life that is clothed in eternal mystery, never to be revealed whilst we inhabit the physical.

Each of us was conceived in the darkness of a reproductive process, encapsulated in a womb where an egg is laid, and sperm rushes to fertilize it. Our conception revealed to the collaborators of our becoming through the vessel called mother, by changes to her biological being. No sooner, we emerge from the womb to the light of the world. A light which shineth undimmed, through the many storms we will encounter as we journey towards an exit as predetermined as our entrance. Yet another darkness clothed in mystery. Who recalls his birth; who can recall his death? The life we have been given but for a time and a season, stems from an eternity of which we know not, grounded in a spirit that breathes life eternal. Eternal life, eternal spirit…

Pause and Harvest...

Envision the promise of reuniting with your loved one, some sweet day.

Unbottled

At times during the grieving process, you might find yourself akin to a bottle of soda shaken, and the cap removed. The shaking is inimical of a buildup of sorrow which becomes uncontainable once the cap is removed. You may find yourself trying to contain the unfolding of this sorrow, by fighting back the tears. But like a shaken bottle of soda, your efforts will be futile. The harder you attempt to fight, the greater the build of pressure which says, release me! We might not all be driven to tears, as part of our grieving process. If you are, know that this is part of the process of coming to terms with your loss and a sowing, a sowing of the seeds for your healing. We cry not because we are weak. We cry because we loved, we were connected, we were invested, because an irreplaceable link in our chain of life has broken away. See your tears as melted ore, working to form a link to repair your chain of life, to make you whole once more.

Pause and Harvest…

Are you bottling up your grief without allowing yourself to be one with your emotions?

Explore channels of expression. Talk to a close friend or confidant. Consider counselling or therapy. Engage in activities that will lift your spirit.

The Mountain Top of Grief

Blessed are those who mourn, they shall be comforted. From whence will your comfort come; via the physical or the spiritual?

When atop the mountain of grief, it is advisable not to make that mountain a dwelling place. The despair of grief will have varying manifestations. In hope and faith, we must journey down this mountain which we did not climb willingly, but rather was parachuted atop of. Like any mountain we ascend or descend, we are likely to slip and slide. We are required to be courageous even while experiencing the weakness grief unfolds on us. Our courage might be spurred on by those who comfort us physically, or through reliance on the spiritual. Both are necessary when we find ourselves atop the mountain of grief. Embrace both as the guiding rope in place to assist you down this challenging mountain.

Pause and Harvest...

Have you ever climbed up a mountain or a hill? If you have, then you will agree that the hardest part of the journey is the ascent. It requires way more effort and energy to climb than it does to descend.

Our grieving is that climb we take. Our descent is the beginning of our healing.

Where are you on this journey?

Grief at Midnight

Distractions are necessary when travelling the road of grief. A single thought, a single 'membering of liza', leads to not just "wata come a mi yeye" but desperate tears of grief. Grief at midnight. Distractions that prompt your mind in another direction, your only solace, relief from being overtaken by your tears. Always so near, so inescapable. Your loss, a most surmounting challenge. You might be yet to ask God why? You are just left to journey through. Why not? Grief comes to us all in this temporal existence. Exiting the mountain top of grief, a journey we can but embrace. Break down like a car if you must. An internal mechanic will restore you to journey on, until your breakdowns cease.

Pause and Harvest...

Consider grief as a lesson in patience. The patience to endure sorrow. The patience to acquiesce to the passage of time when the weight of your loss becomes less burdensome. Patience is required for a wound to heal.

Are you being patient with yourself?

The speck! You and I

When it is asked 'what is man that you should be mindful of him', for those who have ever been aboard an aircraft, suspended thousands of feet above ground, everything below seems insignificant in size. Well, consider man in the context of all that cannot be seen on the ground when suspended in the air above. Indeed, our significance lies in our being seen and the impact we have within our sphere of influence and beyond.

Nonetheless, in the face of all that is, that which is known and unknown, our insignificance remains at large.

Pause and Harvest...

No doubt, the people in our lives who we love and adore are quite significant to us. Death has a way of humbling us; of giving us a perspective we might have ignored or avoided. It challenges us to evaluate our significance in a vast universe where we are like a grain of sand.

Our significance must be viewed through lenses of perspective.

Am I inflating the extent of my significance, manifested in pridefulness?

Immortalized in Memory

Life at times shatters our beautiful vases and leaves us to make what we will of its pieces. Like patchwork, beauty can return. It's up to you and I how we put together those pieces to experience new beauty.

Our experience of new beauty will be reflected in how we remember those we have lost, and not just remember them, but honor all that they meant and represented to us. If we immortalize them, then the grief of our pain will become a little or even much less. We will no longer focus on our broken vase, but recall the vase in its wholeness, immortalized in our memory, an abiding presence, present even though physically absent. Afterall, one's memory unchallenged, is always alive, likened to virtual reality.

Pause and Harvest...

How can you honour the memory of your beloved? Think of something you can do, informed by their favorite pastime or an activity you would engage in together while they were alive. Make it an event!

Limitations

Life happens effortlessly. As effortless as our fingernails growing without us feeling them getting longer. As effortlessly as our hair grows without feeling it being lengthened from our scalp or skin. As effortlessly as our skeleton grows from infancy to adulthood. Life happens effortlessly in the things that are outside of our control, and equally the things necessary for the sustenance of life.

As effortlessly as nature, we see the manifestation of growth, life, and death, without truly observing the actual transition between the varying states. In either state, the extent to which we can prepare for each is limited, limited to that which is known and our limited ability.

In grief, as in life, we must accept our limitations and thereafter embrace the peace that awaits us.

Pause and Harvest...

Usain Bolt, famous Jamaican track star often says, "don't think limits." It is also said that whatever the mind can conceive, we can achieve. While there are elements of truth to each, it doesn't mean we are without limitations. To be without limitations would be akin to a state of perfection.

What are some of your limitations and how best can you navigate them?

Carrying the Cross without Bearing the Load

You, like me, might have been party to a journey which led to the port of grief. Consider the crucifixion story. Jesus was assisted in carrying the cross on which he was to be crucified. Undoubtedly, those who assisted in carrying the cross, while they would have borne its weight, didn't truly experience the load which Jesus carried, beyond the weight associated with the physical cross. Likewise, for us who journeyed the path of sickness with our loved one (s) which brought us to the port of grief, ours was the lesser weight borne. Nonetheless, we can take comfort in the fact that our presence lightened the load of our loved one during their wilderness experience. Whether it was through being their nurse, filling prescriptions, preparing meals, and offering general care, our efforts made their load a bit lighter. Many do not get the opportunity to journey with their loved ones to the port of grief. While there is little consolation given their ultimate demise, we can be assured that they were affirmed in our care and love. In the end, there is so much you and I can do, for each

*of us must do our own living, and even our own dying.
At the port of grief, you are left to wave goodbye as
your loved one boards the vessel towards eternity.*

Pause and Harvest…

Are you a burden bearer? Whose load have you lightened recently?

Could giving of yourself as you grieve assist you along the path of healing?

Death! The Ultimate Manifestation of Healing

We often pray for healing from our afflictions and those things we see real and perceived as not being from God. What if the healing we seek is in the form of death? Are we prepared to embrace it willingly, fearlessly? The living only knows the world we inhabit and as such, strive not easily to relinquish it for a world we know nothing of. If any of us had a real choice, we would choose to live. Yet, we must make peace with the reality that sometimes the healing we seek will come in the form of death. As then, all former things are passed away and behold all things become new, to inhabit a world free of afflictions, free from the experience of sadness and grief, unbounded by time and space.

Pause and Harvest…

Counter intuitive, isn't it? Death as the ultimate healing?

Absurd! No?

Your thoughts…

Next of Kin Grief

There is a juncture that you and I arrive at in our lives that will impact, significantly, our outlook on life. It will thrust many things into perspective. We may have experienced the loss of close friends and family in the past, which may have shaken us and brought us into grief. However, like anything in life, there are levels. The grief you may experience as Next of Kin, is heightened. Your closeness to your loved one demands that the loss is felt more deeply, and as such, your period of mourning extended. There may be those who might not understand why the tears still flow. Well, the cross is yours to bear as Next of Kin. Borne out of love. Your arrival at the destination of consolation unscripted, untimed, undefined. Mourn your deep loss until your shroud of grief is lifted.

Pause and Harvest...

Have you experienced a life altering moment in your living to date? An event that caused you to see things more plainly. An event which realigns your values. One that lays bear the reality of life, its fleeting nature. One that makes you wonder, what really is the point to all of this ('life')?

If you have, recall that moment. How has it shaped you?

Life, the Continuum

As I drove along the Hellshire main road, my eyes caught the flight of a leaf as it was blown by the wind from the limb of a tree. This, though likely unnoticeable by the un-musing mind, caught my attention. It registered in my consciousness the continuum that is life. It said to me in that moment, every living thing transitions. Leaves on a tree pass away, limbs on a tree die, the tree itself is likely to die. Yet, there are trees which are hundreds of years old. No doubt, many leaves, branches even, would have experienced their sunset as a member on the tree of ages, while it continues to live.

Our loved ones are like trees which at an unknown juncture, will die. What we are left with in their transitioning is the sharing of strong roots given to us, which even though a tree dies, its roots are still firmly planted in the ground.

As your grief unfolds, allow the strong roots deposited in you to continue to ground your progression in life.

Secure the roots along the continuum for those you'll leave behind when you arrive at that unknown juncture.

Pause and Harvest...

Many of us will not have offsprings of our own, in whom a piece of us may be implanted. Nonetheless, we can still plant into those who cross our paths, making an indelible impression that helps to shape who they are, and their own becoming.

Are you invested in leaving a positive imprint within your sphere of influence?

Strength to Persevere

Unimaginable grief! In April 2021, a close cousin of mine lost her father during the first week of the month. As if not having to mourn one parent wasn't enough, eleven days later her mom was no more. And as if mourning two parents weren't enough, her grand aunt joined the party to heaven shortly thereafter. Then, I couldn't fathom the insurmountable grief my cousin was in. It was palpably evident. Grief truly has no timetable. Two years later it's Mother's Day. Her tears still flow.

Our grief will endure and will come upon us in moments when we least expect it. We are challenged to summon the spirit of perseverance, amid our grief, to move forward with the assurance that even though grief lives with us, we are strong enough to overcome and carry-on with life.

My grief, your grief, is not a conquering force beyond our strength to subdue it.

Pause and Harvest...

Life presents us with many opportunities to activate our strength. To manifest our resilience. To renew our hope. To affirm our faith.

Will we take these opportunities, even in our moments of weakness?

Comforted

When walking along the journey of grief, there is a blessing to be received in the offering of comfort from those around you. Those who commiserate with you, those who yet close, are not rendered completely grief stricken. Such comfort may come in the form of warm hugs, hands held, prayers said, meals cooked, a general pouring into you, carrying you when you are unable to carry yourself. Embrace this comfort as the manifestation of God coming to you in human form, giving life and meaning to his strength being perfected in your hour of weakness.

Be comforted. Embrace your comforters. Embrace the hands of God.

Pause and Harvest…

It truly takes a village. We are not islands unto ourselves who are self-sustained without reliance on another.

May we not be deceived into believing that we are. If we do, there will be a rude awakening awaiting us, too late in the day.

Letting Go

Relinquishing grief can be compared to our attempt to relieve ourselves of a bad habit which has become second nature to our way of life. The longer we hold onto grief, the more we are likely to separate ourselves from the things which formed part of our routine, prior to being plunged into this emotional state of abeyance.

"Lest we forget," a phrase often used on Remembrance Day in reference to World War II comes to mind. Does letting go mean we forget our loss and our loved ones who have passed? That would amount to an impossible proposition.

Letting go means we recall, but get back into life, our routines, the things we would have continued to enjoy and partake of before grief visited our domain.

Letting go means we continue to dream, to hope, to continue in faith.

Letting go means we accept death as part of our existence, our journey. Indeed, each of us is journeying towards this ultimate end.

Letting go means we know that death is not the end.

Lettings go means we fear not the unknown, since we knew not our beginning, and equally know not our ending.

Letting go means we make peace with our limitations in a limitless universe.

Letting go means we avail ourselves of the 'happenstance' of life.

Letting go means we free ourselves during life's challenges, grief included, to live; to thrive; to experience joy, happiness, love, faith, mercy, and grace. To encounter peace.

Pause and Harvest…

Release! Over time, release yourself from the turmoil of grief. Unlike a given sickness, there is no prescribed medication available. Healing lies in our conscious decision to move ahead, undergirded by the passage of time.

Letting go might not be easy, but it is necessary.

Respite in Grief

After my aunt's funeral, I spent a few days away for a little rest and relaxation. While lying on a beach chair under an almond tree, my mind reflected on the tree, the swing which hung from its branch, the soft wind, and the sand in which the tree was rooted. Picture the almond tree as being you and I, the sand in which it secures itself life, and the swing as the wind of life which takes us forward, sometime backward. Consider now, how rooted you as the tree is, in life, the sand. Are your roots so deep that you will withstand the blows that the winds of life may throw your way? And even if you stumble, are they still so rooted that you will spring afresh?

Give heed to the quality and depths of your roots to sustain you always amidst life's fierce winds and blows; physical, emotional, psychological, spiritual, or otherwise.

Pause and Harvest…

Am I anchored? In what and/or in whom?

One Moment in Time

Modern living. Modern living deceives us into buying into its materialistic essence. It draws us in like pawns in its marketing. Computer algorithms work like mind readers, feeding us with people, places, and things; people we might know, places to go, and things to acquire.

Modern living bombards us with the must haves of life through their marketing campaigns, exploiting our emotions. Like a Drug Enforcement Agent working to entrap a drug baron. We the drug Baron, fall only to shell out our resources, cash, or credit, often on people, places and things which serve only to demonstrate our vanity. Many things we need not. We become hoarders in our quest to acquire more, often losing sight of our substantial, unnegotiable needs; the people, places and things that truly matter. It takes but a moment in time for the materialistic veil of modernity to be lifted from our consciousness to reveal that which truly matters, our unnegotiable needs.

The death of a loved one presents that one moment in time. He who arrives at this moment void of death's intervention is wiser yet.

Pause and Harvest...

Am I a slave to modern living?

Is my vanity beyond visible?

Alive while Alive

The greatest gift that you and I can give ourselves in this life is the gift of living. Just live! Live in a way that fulfils you. Not in an entirely selfish or conceited way, but humbly and peaceably.

For all the misery we are likely to experience along our earthly journey, we should all have that lived experience that helps to balance things out. A lived experience that takes in and gives all the happiness within our grasp to receive and to give.

Just Live. Be alive while alive. Exploit life, before life exploits you.

Pause and Harvest...

What is the state of my living? Am I so caught up in life's routines that I fail to stop and smell the roses? How have I made time for self, without being selfish? Am I making the most of my today since my tomorrow isn't guaranteed?

Round Di Kaanah

For anyone who has ever taken a journey, particularly out of town in Jamaica without fully knowing where to find their intended destination, it is not uncommon for us to ask those we see along the way for directions to where we are going. Typically, such directional guide from those we might encounter, sometimes include an indication that where we are headed is 'jus round di kaanah'. Serendipitously, one may be fortunate to find that their destination is as directed, just round di kaanah. However, in typical Jamaicaness, jus round di kaanah could mean several miles away. We nonetheless accept the directions and hope to find where we are going.

As we journey in life, we never truly know what awaits us round di kaanah. Our fate is as predictable as believing that place we seek, is jus round di kaanah in the Jamaican context. Yet, we must drive on without knowing with certainty what life has in store for us. We accept the directions in faith, hoping that they are accurate and will aide us in finding where we are going.

Whatever fate awaits us round di kaanah, it is our faith which will allow us to journey on, whilst we persevere in the hope of arriving at the place, we set out to be. Never lose sight of faith and hope in journeying round di many kaanahs life has in store for you.

Pause and Harvest...

Are you comfortable, and at peace with the unknown? Do you have anxiety thinking about the unknown?

Here are strategies you might consider for managing your anxiety.

- Therapy (with a medical professional)
- Mediation
- Exercise
- Prayer

Money! Means to a Useful, Useless End

For all the time we commit to chasing the mighty dollar, its usefulness is as unto its uselessness.

Life presents us at intervals with the knowledge that there are priceless things in our experience of life which our riches dare not corrupt, tarnish, prolong or bound. The very soul of these things is beyond the reach of money in relation to its usefulness, thus rendering it useless. Things once lost, good health, true friendship, and time are unlikely to be regained. Herein, money reveals its uselessness, draining away in treatment and medication, seemingly being useful in buying you time, the hope of being restored, only to fail you like the deceiver it reveals itself to be. Alas, in every deceiver there is also some good. Where its usefulness is made manifest, good is found in money. Where its uselessness is made manifest, the promise of its bounty is defeated.

Pause and Harvest…

Money makes the world go round they say. Is this a misnomer?

Am I too focused, beyond reason, on chasing money so much so that I ignore those things which escape its purchasing power?

Momentum

Life is like a muscle that one goes to the gym to build overtime. With each act of commitment, dedication and persistence, the muscle builds and gets stronger, as you commit to making exercise a part of your lifestyle. Any prolonged break from this committed lifestyle will soon find you at a disadvantage. The muscle of life which you were building will lose its momentum and strength, requiring you upon returning to the lifestyle you once committed to, to rebuild the strength of those muscles, to get back to where you were before the break.

After 5 months of not going to the gym as I would previously do at least 3 times per week, I was faced with the reality that my break from life's routine, as I mourned, had resulted in my inability to lift the weights I was lifting with the number of reps, 5 months prior. Thus, forcing me to work my way back to where I was, before interrupted by grief.

Our momentum in life is likely to be disturbed by varying realities, forcing us to regroup and rebuild. The loss of a central family member is one such occasion. Time may heal our wounds, or it might enable us sufficient reprieve to get back into our routine, to regain our momentum and rebuild.

During it all, know that you will know instinctively, when you are ready to get back into the momentum of life before its interruption by grief.

Pause and Harvest...

Is it time to get back on your proverbial horse of life?

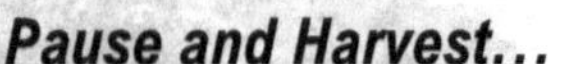

Imprisoned Life

On the balance of probabilities, a law-abiding citizen should have no risk of being imprisoned. Yet so many of us are imprisoned whilst we live. Whether by circumstances beyond our control or those within it, we confine ourselves to a narrow experience of what life has to offer, not recognizing that the time life affords us to be alive is limited. Limited to the moment we are in, the next not being guaranteed. We often spare little thought of the fact that time, in our thrust for life, is our enemy, ticking away at our existence. We put off things we would wish to do for a tomorrow that may never be ours. The prison we confine ourselves to robs us of the authentic embrace of those we hold dear, experiencing the world around us, often overtaken by the routines of life without touching the soul of life. The soul of life which sets us free and at peace, relinquishing the mundane for the sublime. Sublimity itself imprisoned by society's strictures.

It is said "the days of our years are threescore years and ten; and if by reason of strength the be fourscore years, yet is their strength labour and sorrow; for it is soon cut off, and we fly away." Psalm 90:10

Yet not many arrive at threescores; fourscore even. Left we are, mingled in labour, strength, and sorrow in our imprisoned life routines.

May we who remain overcome our imprisonment, routines, and strictures to embrace life's soul, its sublimity; a dress rehearsal for the heaven which we aspire to.

Pause and Harvest...

Am I putting off until tomorrow, that which I can do today?

The Valley

Nature is such a beautiful teacher. I looked down at the valley below Strawberry Hill Hotel and Restaurant (St, Andrew, Jamaica) and it bloomed within my mind's eye that the valley is an exceptionally beautiful place to find oneself. It is refreshing! It's not a place that should leave you tired and drained. The valley is a place of shade, coolness, where you should find refreshing streams, vegetation, peace, and calm.

Often during our valley experiences, that which takes us to this serene place, we are so distracted by our 'situation' that we lose sight of everything that our valley experience presents us with. The emotions that come with grief, a valley experience, is one such distraction. We are so burdened by the loss that we are unable to fully appreciate and embrace the beauty which enfolds us while in our valley of despair.

Embrace the valley experience as one of light as opposed to darkness. A place of great depth and a *height that only the conscious mind can appreciate. A place of restoration beneath your mountain of grief.*

Pause and Harvest...

Am I making effective use of the many streams of refreshment while in the valley of grief?

The Abyss between Life and Death

There is a great abyss between our living and our dying. An abyss which we must fill with the richness of our experiences as we journey towards death. An abyss to be filled by pouring into ourselves and others. An abyss which must be filled with the generosity of our time, our talents, and our treasure to lift those around us, even while we seek to lift ourselves. An abyss which can only be filled when we show up for ourselves and others, like a tide in the harbour causing all ships to rise. An abyss that having been filled by the things which are lasting and everlasting, will never run empty after death has interrupted our purposeful filling of the abyss. An abyss which we must leave behind.

What will we leave in our abyss? Will it have enduring memories for those we must leave behind? What will the span of our abyss tell of our living?

Pause and Harvest…

Is my abyss being filled with those things that will last?

New Every Morning

The breath of life like the fleeting wind, has left your loved one lifeless. Faced with the reality of their demise, going on in the immediate aftermath seems pointless. Nothing makes sense amidst loss. A burden is unleashed that saps your will to go on.

The circle of life which sustains you with the breath life, new every morning, in the aftermath of your loss, propels you forward. Each day that follows, it provides an ounce of grace that gradually fills your basket of perseverance, along the journey of grief. Grace which unloads the burden that, in the days and weeks following your loss, sapped your will to go on.

The circle of life never ceases. For the living, it flows new every morning, accompanied by the fresh morning dew of grace to propel you forward.

Pause and Harvest…

Reflect on your experience and how grace has carried you through times of insurmountable challenges. Now, allow gratitude to overtake you.

Healed, Unhealed Wound

There are some wounds in life which though healed, pressure applied to the area of the wound evokes great sensitivity. The experience of grief is like a healed yet unhealed wound. Healed enough to not be of concern for infection, its rawness covered by scabs. Yet, unhealed to the raw nerves which lie beneath the surface. Nerves easily bothered by the pressure of memory. A realization at times unexpectedly, in a moment when you thought you were restored, only to be undone by the sudden recollection that your loved one is truly gone. Your wound of grief, healed only by the passage of time which makes your loss less immediate, remains unhealed by memories which the passage of time cannot erase.

Pause and Harvest

Our emotional wounds are not unlike our physical wounds. They can be healed, yet unhealed.

What are those healed, yet unhealed wounds you carry?

Abrupt Endings

Many things we started in life will be subjected to abrupt endings. Endings which our minds eyes failed to see coming. Endings which the risk mitigation measures we sought to implement were powerless to dissuade. Endings which our contracts with their many clauses were but as good as the paper they were written on, to preserve contractual obligations and relationships. Endings so abrupt that plans afoot, in spirit or deed fail to come to fruition, rescued only by a testament which overrides your abrupt ending. Abrupt endings unamused by the cinematic performance of our lives, call the production to an end. Unconcerned with intermission and the predictable end as though seated in the theatre.

Abrupt endings reinforce our powerlessness as we grasp as unto the wind, hoping that tomorrow will come. Like the wind fleeing our grasp, such can be our tomorrow. Abrupt endings teach us that even in our planning, it holds the power to change everything. Sometimes for the better, otherwise for the worse.

Abrupt Endings, as certain as our shadow fading away with the evening sunset.

Pause and Harvest...

What if tomorrow doesn't come? What provision should you make for those who must carry-on, when your being fades like the sunset?

For Granted

"Cow neva know di use ah him tail til' him lose it." There is so much we take for granted in our lives. The gift of today, the family members we hold dear. We give no thought while they are with us, that we could lose them. We take for granted that they will always be there. That even when out of sight, they are but a phone call or a drive away. That we will be able to see them, call upon them as we wish. Them not being there is almost unimaginable.

Life in its harsh lessons often jolts us with how immensely we fail to appreciate what we have, when we have it, or even how good we have it. Often, it isn't even the case that we take it for granted or are frugal with our appreciation. The reality is, the living is unconcerned with death, until it presents its unwanted self, amidst our living. More than anything else, it is the void, the absence, the inability to hear your loved one on the other side of a call, see them, touch them, feel them, converse with them, continue to be the beneficiary of their goodwill and them yours.

In the end, our sorrow isn't always demonstrable of the proverb "Cow neva know di use ah him tail til' him lose it", but rather that the cow is robbed of the further and continued use ah him tail, on no account of his own act of having taken him tail fi granted, but simple because forces beyond his control took his tail away.

Pause and Harvest...

Am I appreciating all that I have, and those around me at every opportunity and in every circumstance?

Just Stand

The journey through grief is like going through a storm. In the midst of its strength, akin to the strong wind and heavy rain, the denseness of the atmosphere making visibility a challenge, you may not be able to see your way through. Your clarity is distorted, leaving you unable to see what is on the other side of this inclement stormy weather called grief. Outside the stormy experience, there is also the cold front of grief, which is brought on by a lingering trough which hovers over you like the weather system over a country. Unlike the storm which is akin to the experience in the immediate aftermath, and which is time bound, the cold front of grief is likely to occur more frequently.

Through it all, we must withstand and stand. Withstand the heavy wind and rain of grief's storm, and the cold front of grief. We must muster the strength to stand during it all, to persist through the dense fog which makes the road through grief invisible.

You might have had the experience of stormy weather. Concentrated in one geographic area as you transit, only to be amazed that only meters away it is as dry as chips, while the place left behind was awash.

Just stand! The Storm of grief, its cold front is soon to be in your rear-view mirror. Clearer skies are ahead.

Pause and Harvest...

Reflect on a time when you encountered a significant challenge that you thought you would not overcome. You stand today because you stood then. You'll be okay. Just stand!

Familial Relations

Throughout life's ups and downs, trials and triumphs, we must not lose focus of what truly matters. To borrow a scriptural reference, Micah 6:8 in conveying what the lord requires of us indicates, "to do what is right, love mercy and to walk humbly with your God." Likewise, the importance of good familial relations becomes manifestly important in our moments of trials, even more so than in our moments of triumphs. It is in our trials that we are most weak and vulnerable and need the assistance of those closest to us. A stranger will not do for you in these moments what family will. It is therefore essential for us to appreciate the gift that is our family and to always aim to do what is right, exercise mercy and live humbly with those closest to us. Our triumphs in life are sure to have many relations, our trials will only have those with whom we have maintained good and healthy familial relations, to come to our aid and our rescue.

Pause and Harvest...

Am I at peace with my family? Would my family rally around me in my weakest moments? Would they without a thought come to my aide, to my rescue?

No Spare to the Heir (No Spare Parts)

For almost everything you could think of that man creates, there exist a substitute or a spare part. With the usefulness of money, he can quickly run to the supermarket, the hardware or the parts store and pick up that replacement part that is required. Parts that are widely available. Yet, there are those essentials parts for which there is no substitute or spare for man, even with his creative, inventive genius. Though medical science has advanced in many areas, the created man is yet to crack the code which would allow him to create a spare for a beating heart, a breathing lung, a cleansing kidney, eyes which sees, ears which hears, limbs that work, a tongue to chew, to swallow, and to taste. There is no spare to succeed all these vital organs and body parts of man. No lab in which they can be found. It is left to us to honor the irreplaceable spare-less parts of us, without which we cease to exist.

Pause and Harvest...

Are you invested in your health? Are you taking the necessary precautions as advised by your physician, to mitigate the risk of untreated conditions worsening and affecting your organs for which there are no spare parts? If not, take heed.

Post Traumatic Grief Disorder (PTGD)

The journey of grief can be likened to Post Traumatic Stress Disorder (PTSD). Replacing the stress with grief, we can recoin the stressful experience of death as Post Traumatic Grief Disorder (PTGD).

Like someone affected by PTSD, triggered by recollections of past trauma experienced, so is the person afflicted by PTGD. The experience of grief is a stressor that lives on in the trauma which is the uprooting of one's loved ones from their lives. An abiding presence which is taken away, leaving a void which can never be filled. PTGD carries with the bereaved the images of his/her loved one, particularly those which constantly abides and presents themselves in the mind's eyes like a scene from your favorite movie being replayed constantly in your head. Unlike that movie which evokes warm joyful emotions, the scenes associated with the last moments of your beloved may present itself as a haunting memory; a memory which abides like your shadow beneath the rays of the everlasting sun.

Pause and Harvest…

Reflect! Are there symptoms of PTGD present in your grief journey? Explore coping mechanisms; therapy if needed, or just a listening ear. Do something that brings you joy, that raises a smile as it raises your spirit.

The Noise Within and Without

Life bombards us with a lot of noise. In addition to the noise which occupies our minds internally, we must contend with the noise bombarding us from the outside.

To conquer the noise externally, we must first triumph over the noise we experience internally. Without settling the internal noise, the external noise will serve as a pollutant, leading to much confusion. A state of discombobulation.

Our equilibrium depends on the settling of the many noises within.

The above I believe to be true even in a state of mourning. The noise of the mind ponders many a scenario, leaving you with little resolution to any of them. The many what ifs, and if only. The many had I known, I would have done this, tried that. Maybe things would have turned out differently. These internal ponderings come with the external ponderings of those around you, giving birth to questions which seek to aid their own understanding. Offering at times hypotheses *that threaten to conflate and disturb your own internal noise, adding to the grief already present.*

Ultimately, amidst our grief, we must find that equilibrium by settling the noise within. Only then will we be able to rise above the noise without, to carry on courageously with the assurance that all will be well amid death, our inescapable foe.

Pause and Harvest...

If your internal world is in constant conflict, it will manifest itself like an erupting volcano. Cultivate your peace within. How? Listen to the voice within.

Strength to Uphold Each Other

Enough for today is its own trouble, yet our minds are often taken up, not only with the troubles of today, but the troubles of yesterday, and those we foresee into a tomorrow which may never come.

Have we enough strength for today, to focus on today's trouble? Yet, overwhelmed we often are with the troubles of the past, and even the future.

Strength for today, sufficient to handle the troubles of the present. Strength for today to uphold each other.

The strength we need isn't a selfish strength which is confined to our own unique troubles. The strength we need is that perfect strength which enables us to not only lift ourselves from the sufficient troubles that concerns you and I, but also extends itself to lifting others; to lighten the load of the days trouble which often threatens to buckle us under its weight.

Strength for today, strength to uphold each other. In sickness or in health, in times of better, but more so in times of worse.

Strength for today, strength for tomorrow, strength to uphold each other. Strength to bear one another's burdens.

Pause and Harvest...

It is often said that one cannot pour from an empty cup. Is your cup full enough to pour into someone else without leaving your depleted?

Are you strong enough to be a burden bearer?

57 Completion, 58 New Beginning

Often, the meaning engraved in every experience of our lives escapes us. We exist in an ignorance which is beyond our enlightenment. The universe of knowledge is uncontainable in the minute capacity of the human brain. Yet, search we do, in an effort to put meaning to all things, to aide our understanding, to make sense of, to make peace with, to capture closure which can be like the escapable wind.

Born out of limited knowledge, biblical numeric forced itself to my frontal lobe, causing me to muse on 57, 58. You, my beloved aunt, surrendered 57 for 58; 7 the number of completion, you left us at 57 to begin a new sojourn on what would have been 58, 8 signifying new beginnings.

We too must face a new beginning, releasing our loved one like a student completing an assignment and making its submission, completing the course. The student of life, you, and I, must venture onward to our new beginning; a new course with its own lessons to be taught, lessons to learn as we move ahead. Even *when grief remains with us like a student repeating a class, we must move forward. Life affords us nothing in the past. Hope lies only in the future ahead.*

Move forward to your new beginning, encouraged by cherished memories.

Pause and Harvest...

Your new beginning, without the one you have lost, begins now. Consider the many ways you will make them proud as they smile down at you from the spirit world.

In the End - Nakedness and a Voice

And there we were before our birth, enclosed in the darkness of a womb, within which we hibernated for nine months. The sign of our existence made visible by the enlarged stomach of our carrier; the wonders of modern technology revealing an image of us through ultrasound.

In the beginning, we are pushed out of the darkness of the womb by our carrier. Our gifts, nakedness, and a voice. A nakedness we spend the rest of our lives attempting to clothed. Our voice we spend the rest of our lives trying to find, beyond the scream, the cry which attended our birth.

In the end, but one thing remains. We retain our nakedness, while relinquishing the voice we once had in the beginning.

Oh, how poor we were, yet so rich. Our nakedness, an outward sign of our inherent poverty. Our voice, the wellspring of the riches we carry within us.

Our nakedness and our voice. Abiding companions for the living, but for a moment. In the end, our voice is taken, our nakedness remains. Our nakedness possessed yet, at birth and at death. Our voice, the riches it profited living on, in the hearts and minds we sowed into.

In the end...Centered

Unlike man, the world was built to outlast him.

Don't get lost in the world around you.

Center yourself in the world within.

In the end…Beauty for Ashes

Our lives are subject to shakes, just like the earth itself. May we always regain our bearings after each shake, we experience.

May we be able to pick up the pieces of our world shattered around us.

May we like the potter we are, mold beauty from our ashes as we carry-on.

In the end…. Futility

The world is futile! Our lives are a product of vanity. The vanity of chasing after the worlds many invented conveniences. The vanity of riches, extracted from the poverty of others. The poverty of relinquishing our riches to the vanity the world offers.

In the end, may we conquer our vanity, before it conquers us.

In the End…Peace

May you who mourn walk into an abundance of peace.

A peace that passeth all understanding.

A peace that relieves your troubled mind.

A peace that sets you free to be, to become.

A peace as pure as unspoilt nature.

A peace resplendent like lush green pastures.

In the end...Fortitude

Life would have gotten heavy in the immediate aftermath of your loss. The weight of grief lingers. May you have the grace, willpower, and fortitude to weather the heaviness. On the tail end, may you emerge wiser, not bitter; stronger, not weaker; resolved, not complacent. May your faith be undimmed, your hope energized, and may you be enfolded in the love of those who remain.

In the End...Vision, Mission, Execution

As you carry-on, embrace your rising. Rise to life! An exercise in vision, mission, and execution, outside of which its experience is left to happenstance. Things to be stumbled upon, void of deliberate action and intervention which while not guaranteeing outcomes in absolute certainty, at least guarantees the possibility thereof.

Cheers to life; a function of vision, mission, and execution.

In the End – Scar Tissue

Take a moment to examine your body. How many scar tissues have you counted? Scar tissues that remind you of the events which led to them remaining, as a reminder of bruises you have suffered along your journey.

For most of us, we will recall what led to the scars which have formed part of our skin's tapestry. These scars might not be pleasant to the eyes, but when we patrol them with our fingers as our gaze turns towards them, we are, for some, filled with gratitude that whatever led to the scar (s), we survived it. Some scars are reminders of good times, some of the dangers we escaped.

In as much as our physical scars serve as potent reminders of our life experiences, so too, the emotional scars we carry. The storm of grief is deeply emotional. We carry it with us like a wellspring within. It leaves with us scar tissues. Like the scares visible on our skin, it becomes part of our life's canvas.

The storm of grief will pass. The scar tissue of grief's storm will remain. Embrace it as part of your beautiful mural.

In the End - Parting Words

Having journeyed in Seeds of Tears Harvest of Joy, it is hoped that at this juncture, you found solace in these contemplations as you read them. That they would have assisted you in coming to terms with your loss. That as you read, you were able to align yourself with the emotions, the ponderings, and the philosophizing of the author, as he sought to come to terms with his own loss. It is hoped that the invitation to "Pause and Harvest," would have served as a mechanism throughout this journey in grief exposition, which allowed you to truly harvest your joy, even amidst this difficult life experience.

There are many experiences in life which underscore the likeness of our humanity. Grief is one such experience that equalizes our earthly journey. In grief we are one. Partaking in sorrow, which touches us all at some point along life's voyage.

Journey on! In peace, love, hope, and faith. May the memories of your dearly departed thrust you forward, *empowering you to carry on gracefully, reaping the harvest sown by the tears you have shed.*

In the End…. Psalm 126

"When the LORD restored the fortunes of [a] Zion,

we were like those who dreamed. [b]

2Our mouths were filled with laughter,

our tongues with songs of joy.

Then it was said among the nations,

"The LORD has done great things for them."

3The LORD has done great things for us,

and we are filled with joy.

4Restore our fortunes, [c] LORD,

like streams in the Negev.

5Those who sow with tears

will reap with songs of joy.

6Those who go out weeping,

carrying seed to sow,

will return with songs of joy,

carrying sheaves with them."